E
946
ARN   Arnold, Helen

          Spain:

          PostCards From

K-5 $13.98

VOLUME II IN 12 VOLUME SET

Spain

Helen Arnold

RSVP
RAINTREE
STECK-VAUGHN
P U B L I S H E R S
The Steck-Vaughn Company

Austin, Texas

Published by Raintree Steck-Vaughn Publishers, an imprint of Steck-Vaughn Company

A ZOË BOOK

Editor: Kath Davies, Helene Resky
Design: Jan Sterling, Sterling Associates
Map: Gecko Limited
Production: Grahame Griffiths

Library of Congress Cataloging-in-Publication Data

Arnold, Helen.
    Spain / Helen Arnold.
        p. cm. — (Postcards from)
    "A Zoë Book" — T.p. verso.
    Includes index.
    ISBN 0-8172-4009-8 (lib. binding)
    ISBN 0-8172-4230-9 (softcover)
    1. Spain — Description and travel — Juvenile literature.
    2. Postcards — Spain — Juvenile literature. [1. Spain —
    Description and travel. 2. Letters.] I. Title. II. Series.
    DP43.2.A6 1996
    946–dc20   95–10300
                                                                     CIP
                                                                      AC

Printed and bound in the United States
1 2 3 4 5 6 7 8 9 0 WZ 99 98 97 96 95

Photographic acknowledgments

The publishers wish to acknowledge, with thanks, the following photographic sources:

DDA Photo Library - Cover bl; The Hutchison Library: 6; / John Downman - Cover r, 26; / Gail Goodger - Cover tl; / P.W. Rippon 10; / Maurice Harvey 14; / T. Beddow 20; Robert Harding Picture Library 22; / Earl Young - title page; / Robert Frerck 12, 18; Impact Photos / Bruce Stephens 16; / Michael George 28; Zefa 8, 24.

The publishers have made every effort to trace the copyright holders, but if they have inadvertently overlooked any, they will be pleased to make the necessary arrangement at the first opportunity.

Contents

All the words that appear in **bold** are
explained in the Glossary on page 30.

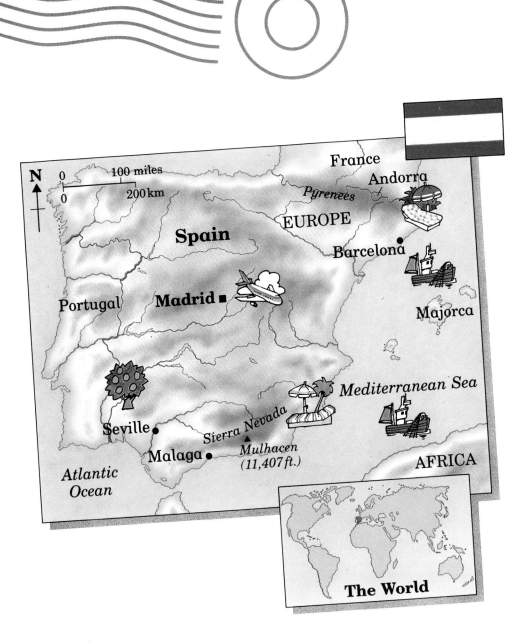

A big map of Spain
and a small map of the world

Dear Kit,

You can see Spain in red on the small map. It is very far away from home. Spain is one of the biggest countries in Europe. The south of Spain is very close to Africa.

Love,

Grant

P.S. Grandpa says that the farther south you go in Spain, the hotter it gets. There is only a narrow **strait** between the south of Spain and the African coast.

In the middle of Madrid

Dear James,

It took about 7 hours for the plane to fly here from New York. Madrid is the **capital** of Spain. There are lots of great things in the stores.

Love,

Maria

P.S. Most people in the stores here speak English and Spanish. Mom says that this is because there are lots of **tourists** in Madrid.

El Retiro park, Madrid

Dear Kathy,

I have a Spanish friend here named Juan. He rushes off for his lunch at one o'clock. All the city stores close for about four hours then. People must take a long time to eat lunch.

Adios (that means "Good-bye"),

Rebecca

P.S. Dad says that El Retiro means "a place to go for a rest." Madrid is noisy and full of traffic. People come to the park for some fresh air.

A fresh fish stand in the market

Dear Nick,

People in Spain like to eat fresh food. This market is full of fish and fruit. Mom gave me some Spanish money called *pesetas*. I bought some strawberries to eat.

Your friend,

Sam

P.S. I drink orange juice when we go out. People make it from fresh oranges. They use machines to squeeze out the juice.

Serving *paella* in Malaga

Dear Emily,

Today I ate a dish called *paella*. It is made with rice, colored yellow with an **herb** called **saffron**. It has chicken, **shrimp**, and tomatoes, all cooked together in a big, flat pan.

Love,

Sarita

P.S. Spanish families eat dinner very late in the evening. Sometimes they go out for a meal with their children at 10 o'clock at night. They also like to eat *paella*.

The AVE train at Seville station

Dear Eddie,

This new Spanish train is called the AVE. Dad says it goes very fast. We hired a car in Madrid. There is not much traffic on the **highways**, but the cities are full of cars.

Your friend,

Ollie

P.S. Grandpa says he likes to go on the slow trains in Spain. They are called *rapidos* (Guess what that means!).

A beach in the south

Dear Amy,

Now we are in southern Spain. The ocean is really warm. It is too hot to sit on the beach all day. Lots of people come here. They stay in vacation houses called *villas*.

Love,

Rosie

P.S. Dad says that the Spanish coastline is more than 2,000 miles long. Spanish people measure in **kilometers**. They say the coast is more than 3,000 kilometers long.

Skiing in the Sierra Nevada mountains

Dear Greg,

Some people go skiing in the mountains in the winter. Lots of Spanish families go to the mountains in the summer, too. It is cooler there. Children here have about eight weeks of vacation in the summer.

Love,

Gerry

P.S. Mom says that the highest mountain in Spain is in the Sierra Nevada.

Taking an evening walk in Las Ramblas, Barcelona

Dear Ali,

This is Barcelona. It is the second biggest city in Spain. It is on the coast and has a big harbor with lots of ships.

Love,

Sanjay

P.S. Mom says that everyone in Spain goes for a walk in the evening. Spanish people call this a *paseo*. Las Ramblas is the favorite place for a *paseo* in Barcelona.

A Spanish soccer team

Dear Janey,

We have seen soccer fields everywhere. Spanish people love sports. They are very good at soccer, tennis, bicycling, golf, and **track and field**. I think they like soccer best.

Love,

Tanya

P.S. Dad says I should see a Spanish game called *pelota*. *Pelota* is the fastest ball game in the world.

A *flamenco* dancer

Dear Rick,

We went to a show last night to see some Spanish dancers. They danced to music played on guitars. The dance is called *flamenco*. At the end, people shouted *"olé."* This means "very good!"

Love,

Roseanne

P.S. Grandma says that every part of Spain has its own special dance. The one for Barcelona is called the *sardana*.

Girls dressed up for a *fiesta*

Dear Lewis,

It was a special day here yesterday, a **festival**. Spanish people call it a *fiesta*. These festivals are held all over Spain. Sometimes they end with fireworks.

Your friend,

Leroy

P.S. Mom says that most people in Spain are **Christians**. Many of the *fiestas* start with a big parade through the town to the church.

The Spanish flag, flying over a bank in Madrid

Dear Val,

The red and yellow colors on the flag stand for two old Spanish kingdoms. Long ago the queen of Castile married the king of Aragon. Spain then became one big country.

Love,

Gabriella

P.S. Dad says that the king and queen of Spain do not rule the country now. People choose their leaders. Spain is a **democracy**.

Glossary

Capital: The town or city where people who rule the country meet. It is not always the biggest city in the country.

Christians: People who believe in the teachings of Jesus

Democracy: A country where the people choose the leaders they want to run the country

Festival: A time when people celebrate something special or a special time of year

Herb: A plant used in medicines, to flavor or color foods, or to make something smell good

Highway: A large main road that helps people get from one place to another more directly

Kilometer: A measure of length

P.S.: This stands for Post Script, which means "to write after." A postscript is the part of a card or letter that is added at the end, after the person has signed it.

Saffron: Part of a flower used to color and flavor foods

Shrimp: A small sea animal with a long, thin body covered with a shell

Strait: A narrow stretch of ocean that separates two pieces of land

Tourist: A person who is taking a vacation away from home

Track and field: Sports such as running, high jump, and long jump

Index